IVIES

AN ILLUSTRATED GUIDE TO VARIETIES, CULTIVATION AND CARE, WITH
STEP-BY-STEP INSTRUCTIONS AND OVER 150 INSPIRING PHOTOGRAPHS

Hazel Key

Consultant: Stephen Taffler
Photography by Jonathan Buckley

southwater

This edition is published by Southwater
an imprint of Anness Publishing Ltd
108 Great Russell Street, London WC1B 3NA
info@anness.com

www.southwaterbooks.com; www.annesspublishing.com

If you like the images in this book and would like to investigate
using them for publishing, promotions or advertising, please visit
our website www.practicalpictures.com for more information.

© Anness Publishing Ltd 2015

A CIP catalogue record for this book is available from the British Library.

Publisher: Joanna Lorenz
Editor: Margaret Malone
Designer: Caroline Grimshaw
Production Controller: Pirong Wang

PUBLISHER'S NOTE
Although the advice and information in this book are believed to be accurate and true at the time
of going to press, neither the authors nor the publisher can accept any legal responsibility or liability
for any errors or omissions that may have been made nor for any inaccuracies nor for any loss,
harm or injury that comes about from following instructions or advice in this book.

■ HALF TITLE PAGE
Hedera colchica 'Dentata'
■ FRONTISPIECE
Hedera algeriensis 'Monty'
■ TITLE PAGE
Ivy growing up around a statue

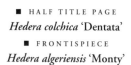

■ LEFT
Tendrils of ivy creep across a wall
■ OPPOSITE LEFT
Hedera colchica species
■ OPPOSITE RIGHT
Hedera colchica 'Sulphur Heart'

Please return / renew by date shown.
You can renew at: **norlink.norfolk.gov.uk**
or by telephone: **0344 800 8006**
Please have your library card & PIN ready.

Contents

Introduction

*I*vies are very adaptable and decorative foliage plants that are used as houseplants and garden plants worldwide. They are evergreen and hardy, and their leaves display a wonderful variety of shapes, colours and sizes. Ivies have a very ancient lineage and still exist in the wild as they have for over ten thousand years. Many of the ivy plants we use today developed from the wild plant through the spontaneous sporting to different clones, which gardeners then selected and propagated. This creates an ever-changing availability of plants with various kinds of leaf shape and patterning.

Whether you need plants to scramble over a wall, an evergreen plant to grow in a window box all year round, or romantic tendrils growing up a statue, ivies are an excellent choice. Easy to grow, they hide the ugly and make splendid features in their own right.

■ RIGHT
Frost settles on the leaf edges of this *Hedera helix.*

Discovering ivy

The ivy is one of the best-known, most popular foliage plants. It is sold in florists, garden centres, nurseries and even supermarkets all year round.

Characteristically good-tempered, ivies do not succumb immediately if they are accidentally neglected. Indeed, some ivies sold as indoor plants can be hardened off and planted in the garden. If in doubt, though, it is safer to buy one that has been specifically grown as a hardy garden plant. Plants bought from nurseries in pots and grown under hardy conditions can usually be planted outside all year round.

Ivies can be used as climbers or trailers, but with judicious pruning they can also be grown in the border. Furthermore, it is easy for amateurs to propagate their own plants: each ivy can yield dozens of potential new plants each year.

The origin of ivies

Ivies originated from the ancient, wild ivy plants that grew in woodlands and hedgerows in Europe, primarily Great Britain, and to a lesser extent in Asia and North Africa. In the wild, ivies tended to mutate different clones, with unusual leaf formations and variegations, which gardeners then propagated by taking cuttings of the variable shoots and growing them as individual plants. Ivies first began to be grown commercially in Britain in the 18th century, appearing in the nurserymen's catalogues of the day.

The eminent Swedish botanist Carolus Linnaeus, writing in his *Species Plantarum* about binomial nomenclature in 1753, gave ivy the botanical name *Hedera helix*, thereby raising it to the status of a superior garden plant.

Ivies in the garden

The middle of the 19th century saw the advent of weekly and monthly gardening magazines, which enabled gardeners at every level to read about

contemporary horticulture. Much was
written about ivy, and its popularity
increased greatly as a result.

In England at that time, Shirley
Hibberd, the editor of the magazine
Floral World, and owner of a private
collection of ivies and different
clones, wrote a comprehensive book
on the subject. He summoned all his
knowledge of history, poetry and
even Greek mythology for quotations
on ivy, and illustrated it throughout
with numerous woodcuts and colour
plates, creating a very substantial
book. Published in 1872, *The Ivy,
A Monograph* was so successful that a
second edition was printed in 1893.
This book became the standard work
on ivy for the next century, and is a
collector's item today.

By the beginning of the 20th
century, ivies were widely grown in
gardens, conservatories and indoors.
However, the outbreak of World War I
in 1914 interrupted most gardening
activities in Europe. After World
War II, there was a revival of interest in
plants as attractive homes and gardens
once again became desirable and
achievable. Ivies in the wild continued
to develop a variety of variable clones.
In some cases, these have then been
propagated and grown as individual
plants by gardening enthusiasts.

Ivies in the United States

Ivies are not native to the United States, but were introduced by the early British settlers in the 18th century. *Hedera helix* had to acclimatize itself to American soil, which is not as calciferous as British soil, and in doing so, it sported more and more clones as it adjusted to the new conditions. In 1921, a new clone appeared in the United States, very different from its predecessors. It was named *Hedera helix* 'Pittsburgh', and became the forerunner of the houseplant ivy. Unlike the native *H. helix,* it had a small, thin leaf, a ramulose or much-branching habit, and it did not grow into adult form, nor did it flower or berry – it was the ideal houseplant ivy. This plant and further clones from it were put into mass production and became a million-dollar industry in the United States, being exported from the USA to Europe and Britain, where houseplants were becoming fashionable following World War II.

Classifying ivies

In 1973, the American Ivy Society was formed, followed by The British Ivy Society in 1974. For both organizations, the priority was to ensure the correct nomenclature of ivies and to establish the publication of regular journals on the subject.

The Royal Horticultural Society in Britain, recognizing a resurgence of interest in ivies among its members, held an invited trial of the plants. About 200 ivies were planted at the Society's garden at Wisley, Surrey, England, in order to observe the ivies growing side by side. This showed exactly what problems lay ahead in trying to name and describe correctly all of the clones. Some of the American non-flowering clones looked extremely attractive as garden plants, though it was difficult to determine their hardiness during the course of the trial. When it was over, cuttings of the plants were rooted and transferred to the National Trust Gardens at Erddig, in North Wales, to establish a National Collection.

Dispelling myths about ivy

From time to time, people ask if ivy is poisonous – the answer is no. In fact, farmers have been known to use ivy as a cure for certain sick animals, and in times of fodder shortage they feed cut ivy to their cattle. The question arises because in the United States there is a plant commonly known as 'poison ivy'. This plant (botanically named *Rhus radicans*) causes an itchiness and swelling after contact with the skin, but it is not a true ivy.

Ivy is also mistakenly thought to kill trees. In its juvenile form, ivy tends to grow along the ground and climb the nearest upright object in its path, which in the wild is likely to be a tree, in order to reach the light. It climbs by putting out tiny, clinging rootlets. These are not true roots as they do not penetrate the bark, but 'hold fast' the ivy to prevent it from blowing about in the wind. The normal growing roots come from just below the joints in the ground.

Once the ivy reaches the top of the tree, it no longer puts out clinging rootlets, but instead develops bushy, non-climbing shoots, then proceeds to flower and berry each year.

If the ivy has climbed up an old or diseased tree, turning adult in the process, it becomes very bushy and top-heavy, and can cause a tree to break or become uprooted in a gale. This is perhaps one of nature's ways of felling old trees and making room for younger ones. If you choose to grow an ivy up a tree in your garden, use one of the modern ramulose (self-branching) types that are less likely to turn adult. Or, if you use one of the older types, prune the ivy hard when it gets halfway up the tree, to keep it within bounds.

■ LEFT
The larger-leaved adult growth mixes with the juvenile growth on this *H. helix* 'Cypria'.

■ RIGHT
Ivy climbs using clinging rootlets that do not penetrate the bark of a tree.

Ivy makes an excellent covering for a structure, such as a wall, but it is often considered risky to grow against brickwork. In the case of a well-maintained wall or new building, ivy will not cause damage to the bricks or penetrate cement; indeed, if you prune it regularly, as you would other plants, it will actually protect the wall from the elements. However, it is true that ivy can damage an old building. Until the ivy is disturbed, it may even help keep the building together, but the action of pulling away the plant may cause the some of the old brickwork to come with it.

Ivies for ornamental uses

Ivies have always been in great demand as garden plants, and they are being used in increasingly imaginative ways. One of their great features is their ability to cover and conceal unsightly structures or eyesores. They grow happily in the open garden, in containers outdoors, or in the house or conservatory. Best of all, growing ivies is inexpensive, because you can always use cuttings of existing plants to increase your stock. When you have taken cuttings, it is best to pot them on and keep them in a frame until they grow to a decent size.

Garden and house walls

The classic situation for ivy is growing up a wall. If you have a sunny wall, plant *Hedera helix* 'Buttercup' against it, and the results will be spectacular. On a wall that gets no sun, the delightful *Hedera helix* 'Goldheart', with green-edged, gold-centred leaves, will grow well and keep its colour. In fact, it is the only gold ivy that does not need sun to keep the colour variegation. Ivies growing up a bare wall at intervals are eye-catching, but do not plant them too closely, or they will cover each

■ ABOVE AND OPPOSITE BELOW RIGHT Ivy can turn almost any object in the garden into an attractive feature, as with this unused well and watering can.

■ LEFT *Hedera helix* 'Buttercup' makes a perfect backdrop to the pink and red tones of these 'Coleus', grown as summer bedding only.

other. You will also need to leave space to clip between them. Big-leaved species look particularly attractive trained up a trellis, but the stems will need to be tied in place because they do not hold fast along their stems.

Always make sure that the ivy is not allowed anywhere near roof gutters. Cut it back each year before it gets anywhere near them.

Border plantings

Some garden landscapers use mixed ivies as effective mass bedding plants, though they require pruning once or twice a year to stop them from growing into each other. Ivy also makes excellent edging to a flower border, providing an attractive

'finishing touch'. They can also be grown along the edge of a garden path, along steps, or planted on a terrace garden to great effect. By edging each stepped border of a terrace, the ivy will create a stunning cascade effect.

Ground cover

Ivy makes excellent ground cover, and can completely cover large areas relatively quickly. One of the best ivies for ground cover is *Hedera*

■ ABOVE
'Chicago Variegated' adds interest around the base of the statue, and softens and complements the stone.

hibernica. Many *Hedera helix* cultivars are also suitable, especially the dark green 'Ivalace' or 'Shamrock'.

Ivy is a good substitute for grass where grass will not thrive, such as in dense shade. It can also be planted on a bank instead of grass: it holds the soil in place better, and eliminates mowing in a difficult situation.

Ivy (shown here with campanula) makes an elegant trailing plant for hanging baskets.

Training for effect

Ivy can be grown into attractively shaped specimen plants, perfect for improving a dull corner, or for accentuating other plants. They can be trained to create striking standards or topiary, and are effective growing up a tripod to bring height to the border. In the winter, fill 15cm (6in) pots with compost (soil mix) and plant them with five rooted cuttings of *Hedera helix* clones, especially the silver 'Glacier' or green and gold 'Goldheart', 'Anne Marie' and 'Chester'. For green varieties, try 'Manda's Crested', 'Cristata' and 'Jasper'. Small-leaved varieties for small arrangements include 'Spetchley', 'Duckfoot' and 'Adam'. This last variety has prettily marked cream edges. Stand the pots on a bench in a cold greenhouse or tunnel. The following spring, add a tripod of canes to each pot, train the growth up them and stand the containers in the garden.

Ivy can also be trained along the separate arches of uncovered tunnels (sun-heated pits), completely covering them within a few years. This is then an ideal spot to plant shade-loving hardy ferns that suffer from scorching in direct sunlight.

Indoor ivy

Ivy has a long history of being grown as an indoor plant. It was extremely popular in Victorian times throughout the home. Rooms were decorated with long trails of ivy draped around windows, doorways, pictures and mantelpieces. The adult forms were made into small potted

You can train ivy along trellises or above a doorway for shade and privacy.

shrubs, complete with berries, to enliven the parlour.

Ivies are also very good plants for the cold conservatory, where they thrive. Again, ivy was popular in Victorian conservatories, where it was commonly grown up arches and pillars. Specimen plants look very striking accompanied by evergreen hardy ferns. Choose complementary flowers such as pots of primroses and winter-flowering pansies. Adding potted cyclamen will give extra colour to the collection in autumn.

Ivies can suffer in the heat. Unless your conservatory has blinds, it is best to take the plants outdoors in summer, placing them in a shaded spot. In autumn, repot the plants and give them a good trim, then return them to the conservatory, keeping the windows open for a week or two so that the plants can gradually adjust to the new conditions.

Containers

Ivies make excellent container plants, particularly for winter arrangements, as they are both evergreen and most are hardy. Planted as a permanent feature at the edge of a window box, they make a good foil to wallflowers or pelargoniums. Ivies are also attractive in hanging baskets. The baskets can be left outside all winter in a sheltered spot, but if you have a greenhouse or tunnel (sun-heated pit) it is best to use that for the coldest months in case the root balls freeze.

The foliage of ivies is ideal for flower arrangers, who often like to grow their own material. To obtain long, straight stems, it is best to plant the ivy in hanging pots or baskets, letting the plants trail down over the edges. The large-leaved *Hedera colchica* 'Sulphur Heart', *Hedera algeriensis* 'Gloire de Marengo', 'Marginomaculata' and *Hedera hibernica* are all good for large pedestal arrangements.

■ BELOW
A cascade of ivy over this portico makes a magnificent evergreen feature.

Ivy botany

All ivy species are native to Europe, including Britain, North Africa, and Asia, growing mainly in light woodland and hedgerows. Although ivy enjoys much popularity in the United States, it is not in fact native to the Americas.

Dr Berthold Seeman, a German botanist who trained at Kew Gardens in England, did much to further the understanding of ivies. In his review of the genus *Hedera* in 1864, published in the *Journal of Botany*, he designated three species of *Hedera*: *H. helix*, *H. algeriensis* and *H. colchica*. He also explained that although ivy seems to be a hairless plant, it does in fact have hairs on the underside of the leaves and on the stalks of the berries (visible only with a strong magnifying glass). The hairs, coupled with chromosome counting, are one of the chief methods still used today as a means of identification.

By the beginning of the 20th century, another two species were identified, making five in total. They were *H. nepalensis* and *H. rhombea*. Other species have been identified by researchers in recent times, though not all authorities agree as to these further classifications.

Stages of growth

The English native ivy, *Hedera helix,* still grows in the wild today. These plants show best how the unusual botanical phenomenon of dimorphism occurs, with two distinct stages of growth often evident on one plant.

When ivy is first potted up from rooted cuttings, it is in the attractive juvenile form with three- to five-lobed leaves, and it grows in a vining fashion, clinging with little hook-like rootlets (holdfasts). It is very easy to propagate when young.

When it has grown for at least two years, and has climbed up a post or tree, ivy can enter its adult form: the leaves gradually lose their decorative shapes, become plainer, and it is said to be arborescent. The stems thicken, and the plant takes on a shrub-like appearance. The different clones will have reverted to their original species. Every year from this stage on, the plant will produce blooms from summer onwards, followed by berries.

■ LEFT
Correct classification is hindered by the same plant having more than one name. *Hedera colchica* has had five names.

■ RIGHT
On mature ivy throughout winter, berries are an important source of food for birds.

Flowers

Ivy flowers appear as clusters of tiny yellow cup-shaped blooms that are sweetly perfumed and heavy with nectar, attracting butterflies, wasps, and other insects. The flowers are usually covered with these insects until every bit of pollen is gone and the flowers are thoroughly fertilized to ensure berry production. Generally, the American self-branching clones deriving from 'Pittsburgh' are not dimorphic and do not flower – these clones can be propagated only by taking cuttings.

Berries

After the flowering stage, ivies produce berries that ripen in winter. The berries are spherical and usually black, but are sometimes orange or yellow. After the birds digest the berries, they then excrete the seed that was contained inside the berry, ensuring that the ivy seeds are sown over a wide area. Interestingly, *Hedera helix* seedlings do not resemble the clone on which the berries were borne, but are almost invariably green and show normal five-pointed leaves. Consequently, new clones are raised from cuttings not from sown seed.

SOME USEFUL TERMS

Adult – the stage of growth of a plant when mature (for ivies, after two or three years, although not all reach this stage). Mature ivies produce flowers and berries, and usually unlobed leaves.

Clone – a plant derived from one original plant by vegetative propagation.

Cordate – a heart-shaped leaf with a pointed tip, rounded base and a deep cleft at the centre.

Cultivar – a plant that has been propagated vegetatively, retaining all the original characteristics.

Dimorphism – the occurrence within a plant of two distinct forms, such as the juvenile and adult stages in ivy.

Genus – a botanical group that contains one or more related species. *Hedera* is the name of the genus to which all ivies belong.

Juvenile – the early stage of growth. Juvenile ivies creep or climb with self-clinging rootlets, and generally have leaves with three to five lobes. They do not produce flowers or berries.

Lobes – the divisions of a leaf at its edge, which do not go beyond the mid-rib.

Pinching out – a horticultural term for removing the tip of a shoot with the finger and thumb to prevent the shoot from growing any longer, and to instead encourage the stem to send out side shoots at the leaf joints.

Ramulose – plants with shoots arising from every node, often also referred to as self-branching. This describes the modern form of ivy, first seen in the United States, which originally sported from *Hedera helix*.

Rootlets – adventitious holdfasts, not true roots.

Sinus – the gap or division between two lobes. An arrow sinus indicates a deep cleft with the lobes close to each other. A shallow sinus indicates a broad gap with lobes wide apart.

Species – a category in plant classification consisting of plants within the same genus that have natural characteristics which enable them to be identified from other species in that same genus.

Sport – a mutation of plant form which occurs naturally where the plant changes habit and style from the original parent plant.

Ivy species

The following pages give examples of the ivy species within the genus *Hedera*. From these relatively simple beginnings comes the constantly changing range of varieties and clones that is especially true of *H. helix*.

■ RIGHT
HEDERA ALGERIENSIS

Native to Algeria, this ivy has very large glossy green leaves on wine-red stems. There is much discussion surrounding the ivy 'Gloire de Marengo', which many consider to belong to *H. canariensis*.

■ BELOW
HEDERA AZORICA

For some time, this was considered to be part of *H. canariensis*. It was not until 1988 that specific status as a species was proposed. Endemic to the non-desert Azores Islands, this dark green, five- to seven-lobed species makes an excellent wall ivy.

■ ABOVE
HEDERA CANARIENSIS

First described by Willdenow in 1808, this is native only to the mountains of the Canary Islands. Lost to cultivation, it was only found again in the 1970s. The large leaves are cordate three-lobed with shiny early growth becoming a duller green when it matures. Not hardy, but could be grown in a sheltered position. The revision of the species by McAllister, Mills and Rutherford in 1983 has been followed in this book.

■ RIGHT

HEDERA HELIX

Named by the botanist Carolus Linnaeus, the common ivy has dark green, shiny, three- to five-lobed, medium-sized leaves. During cold weather, the leaves often turn a deep bronze-purple colour. Very hardy, it needs alkaline soil for good growth. Extremely variable, most ivies grown in the garden and as houseplants belong to this species.

■ ABOVE

HEDERA COLCHICA

This species was given its definitive description by the German botanist Kaspar Koch in the mid-19th century. A Persian ivy with large, dark green, shiny, heart-shaped leaves with smooth edges, it is a hardy plant. It provides excellent ground cover, as the leaves are closer together than the popular cloned *H. colchica* 'Dentata' types. The named clone 'My Heart' is considered the type specimen.

■ LEFT

HEDERA CYPRIA

This has a medium-sized ovate leaf, with conspicuous grey veining, and red stems. It is found in the Troodos mountains of Cyprus. Good as a specimen plant and for planting against walls.

■ LEFT
HEDERA RHOMBEA

This Japanese ivy has undergone several name changes, but has finally assumed the name given by the Dutch botanist Miquel, in 1863. This species looks rather delicate, but is in fact quite hardy. It has small to medium-sized, dark green, heart-shaped leaves, heavily veined grey.

■ ABOVE
HEDERA HIBERNICA

Named by Petzold and Kirchner in 1864, this species grows on the western seaboard from the Straits of Gibraltar to south-west Scotland. There are many forms from these areas, but British plants are very similar to *H. helix*, which has caused much discussion over whether or not *H. hibernica* should be considered a separate species. It has medium, mid-green leaves, which turn bronze in cold weather, and are mainly pointed and three- to five-lobed, though many forms do not have this typical ivy-shaped leaf. Very vigorous and robust, this species includes many 19th-century cultivars and the so-called 'Irish Ivy', *H. hibernica*. The species is used extensively in horticulture for large landscape plantings.

■ LEFT
HEDERA MAROCCANA

Named by Hugh McAllister in recent times, this ivy is native to the Middle Atlas Mountains in Morocco. There are two forms: *H. maroccana* 'Spanish Canary', with medium-sized to large, three- to five-lobed, emerald-green, shiny leaves with red veins, ruby petioles and red stems; and the slower-growing *H. maroccana* 'Morocco' (shown here), with smaller, wider, three-lobed leaves.

■ LEFT
HEDERA MADERENSIS

For a long time considered a variety of
H. algeriensis, it was not until 1988 that
this was put forward for consideration as
a distinct species. It is named after the
islands of Madeira, where it grows in the
wild, and was first suggested by Kaspar
Koch in 1869. It has medium-sized
to large, dull, mid-green, three-lobed
leaves, with raised veins and red stems.

■ LEFT AND RIGHT
HEDERA NEPALENSIS
VAR. *SINENSIS*

Established as a distinct species
by Professor Tobler and Alfred
Rehder in the first half of the
19th century, this is commonly
referred to as 'Chinese Ivy'.
During the juvenile stage, the
species has deep yellow-green,
slightly glossy veins that are
scarcely visible; the sharp-tipped,
three-lobed leaves are deeply
cordate, with deep sinuses
and upswept lateral lobes.

Leaf shape and colour

The range of ivy leaf shape and colour is one of ivy's most endearing qualities. Be it a glorious golden colour or a frilled edge, there is an ivy to suit all situations and tastes.

■ LEFT
DENSE SILVERY GROWTH

For small silver, irregular three-lobed leaves, *Hedera helix* 'Ardingly' is a good choice. It is self-branching, with very dense growth. Suitable for hanging baskets and containers.

■ ABOVE RIGHT
GOLDEN ARROW-SHAPED

The small leaves of *Hedera helix* 'Lightfingers' are gold and arrowhead-shaped, with three lobes and a very clear-cut outline. Good for hanging baskets and as houseplants.

■ RIGHT
CREAMY WHITE VARIEGATION

Hedera helix 'Anne Marie' has attractive leaves with creamy white edges and grey-green centres. They are medium-sized and three- to five-lobed. Useful for pillar plants, hanging baskets and containers.

■ ABOVE
CLASSIC GOLD COLOURING

Hedera helix 'Goldchild' has medium-sized, gold leaves with grey-green centres, and three to five lobes, with a long central lobe. Older leaves can grow quite large. Good in a hanging basket, or as a pillar ivy or houseplant.

■ LEFT
CORDATE

Leathery and dark green,
the medium- to large-sized
leaves of *Hedera hibernica*
'Deltoidea' are cordate at
the base, with basal lobes
overlapping when mature.
This leaf shape is sometimes called
'heart-shaped' or 'sweetheart' in
the USA. It grows stiffly upright,
and is a superior architectural
plant for the garden.

■ LEFT
NON-CLINGING AND UPRIGHT

Several ivies, such as *Hedera helix*
'Erecta' (shown here), are non-
climbing, and form upright,
bushy growth. In this plant,
the compact dark green leaves
are three-lobed or unlobed;
flowers and berries are never
present. Its stiffly upright growth
suits a rock garden or shrub
border, but it needs a support
cane when growing.

■ ABOVE
FRILLED WITH PINK EDGES

Medium-sized, undulating, green leaves with
prominent veins, as shown here with *Hedera helix*
'Melanie'. The leaf margins have narrow pink
crimped edges, which gives the rounded leaf a
frilly appearance. This unusual frilled effect is an
attractive variation on the curly-leaf type. Makes a
good houseplant or specimen plant for a container.

■ LEFT
BIRD'S FOOT-SHAPED

The grey-green *Hedera helix*
'Pedata' is known as the 'bird's
foot ivy' because of its leaf shape:
five-lobed, with a long central
lobe and lateral lobes
almost at right
angles to it. Suitable
for growing up walls.

Plant Directory

Hedera helix is the most numerous species of ivy, and is the most popular ivy for growing in gardens or as a houseplant. The range of clones to choose from in this species make it the most variable and interesting. For this reason, the following directory is a showcase only of that species, though in the Other Recommended Ivies section at the back of the book, examples of other species are given.

The expression three- to five-lobed refers to the number of points on a leaf: when young, a leaf may have only three lobes, but this may increase to five as the plant matures. Typical leaf colour is given, though it is not unusual for a great variety to exist, depending on soil and climatic conditions.

■ ABOVE RIGHT
'AMBROSIA'

Slightly curled and twisted small leaves make this an interesting ivy, but it is very slow-growing. It was found at the Neuberg Monastery, Heidelberg, in Germany, as a sport from 'Gertrud Stauss'. The leaves are light green with light yellow-cream variegation towards the edges. Suitable for rock gardens.

■ RIGHT
'ANGULARIS AUREA'

A yellow ivy that turns adult by the time it is five years old. New foliage is bright yellow, but old foliage is mottled and green. Good for growing up walls, fences and pillars, and for training into a tree ivy.

■ RIGHT

'BRUDER INGOBERT'

This ivy was a mutation from 'Glacier', and was selected by Brother Ingobert at the Neuberg Monastery Nurseries, Heidelberg, in Germany. The leaves are deep grey-green, thinly edged creamy white, and are variable in shape. Fairly hardy, it can be used as a houseplant or for a hanging basket, or on low walls. It is a branching ivy, with purple-red stems. It has medium-sized, three- to five-lobed leaves, but the lower lobes are not always distinct.

■ ABOVE

'BOSKOOP'

A mutation from 'Green Ripple'. The shiny, dark green, medium-sized leaves have three to five lobes, all pointing forward, giving a claw-like appearance. The sinuses are narrow, with leaf edges raised at the cleft, giving a frilled appearance. Makes a good houseplant.

■ RIGHT

'BILL ARCHER'

A good houseplant needing a loam-based compost (soil mix), this has a short-jointed habit. The dark grey-green small to medium-sized leaves, with white veins, are very slender, curved and unlobed, quite unlike a typical ivy leaf. It looks very attractive in a hanging pot.

■ ABOVE
'CATHEDRAL WALL'

A green ivy similar to *Hedera helix,* collected and used as a garden plant by Mr A. Rosenboon, the gardener at Washington Cathedral in Washington DC, in the United States. Its habit is short-jointed and self-branching with three-, sometimes five-lobed, medium-sized leaves in mid-green. A good houseplant ivy where a plain green is required.

■ LEFT
'CAVENDISHII'

The three-lobed, pointed leaves are angular when young, less so with maturity. The leaf centre is grey-green, occasionally breaking through to the irregular edge of cream-yellow. It grows well on low walls, over archways and as a pillar plant.

■ LEFT
'BUTTERCUP'

This ivy has a very beautiful gold colour and looks best on a wall where it gets sunlight for at least half of the day and is grown in limy (alkaline) soil. It has medium-sized, five-lobed leaves, and is one of the varieties that does turn adult in due course, probably because it is always grown in good light. It should be planted immediately on purchasing into a loam-based compost (soil mix) or straight into the garden against a wall. It is not good as a houseplant; several houseplant clones have been sold as this variety, but they do not keep a good colour and are probably not 'Buttercup'.

■ BELOW
'COCKLE SHELL'

A self-branching sport from 'California'. The medium-sized leaves, which are attractively veined, are untypical for ivy: they are unlobed and appear almost circular, but occasionally three to five vestigial lobes appear. The upturned leaf edges are mid-green, with light purple stems. Good for hanging baskets and as an edging plant.

■ ABOVE
'CHICAGO VARIEGATED'

This is a pale yellow and green sport of 'Chicago', and has smaller leaves than 'Pittsburgh', from which 'Chicago' originated. It is self-branching and has a good colour if grown in loam-based compost (soil mix), but if grown in soilless compost (planting mix), many green trails appear and spoil the look of the plant. The medium-sized leaves are three- to five-lobed, with the centre lobe longer and with the basal lobes sometimes showing. It is very good for planting in hanging baskets and containers, especially if grown as a specimen plant.

■ RIGHT
'CONGESTA'

One of a group of
upright, non-clinging
ivies widely grown in
Europe. It has small,
three-lobed cupped
leaves crowded on
stiff stems. The whole
plant stem seems to
grow upright from the
top joint, and spread
from the base of the
plant, making it a very
unusual ivy. Good
for rock gardens,
ground cover and as
a specimen plant for
an architectural focal
point in the garden.

■ ABOVE
'CONGLOMERATA'

This is from the same group of non-
clinging ivies as 'Congesta' and 'Erecta',
though not a sport of either. The stems
become curved branches covered with
small, dark green, leathery leaves that
cup and curl. It is a very good plant
for a large rock garden, creating a low-
growing bush that climbs down in tiers.

■ LEFT
'CURVACEOUS'

A variegated sport
from 'Manda's
Crested'. The curly,
medium-sized three-
lobed leaves have
cordate bases, grey-
green centres and
creamy white edges.
The leaves develop a
reddish tinge in cold
weather. Ideal for
hanging baskets,
pillars or climbing
up a cane or stick in
a pot as a houseplant.

■ RIGHT
'DRAGON CLAW'

This attractive ivy has
large, broad, five-lobed
leaves, curling
downwards, with
closely fluted edges
that turn red in
winter. Good for
growing up walls
and ground cover.

■ LEFT
'DUCKFOOT'

Another small-leaved, self-
branching modern ivy from the
United States. It appeared in the
nursery of Ballas and Tillender
at Bound Brook, New Jersey, as
a sport from 'Merion Beauty'.
'Duckfoot' was registered with the
American Ivy Society in 1978. It
has a bushy habit, with medium-
sized, light green, three-lobed
leaves, with shallow sinuses, and
purple stems. It winters outside,
provided it is not planted in
soilless compost (planting mix).
'Duckfoot' makes a good edging
plant for a border, and is also
suitable as a houseplant.

■ LEFT
'ERECTA'

This plant is the most handsome of the non-clinging ivies. The medium-sized leaves are three-lobed, occasionally unlobed, growing on stiff upright stems. It does not climb, but grows upright on thickened stems. If the plant is supported by a single stake it can grow as high as 1.8m (6ft), and makes a plant of great architectural merit, especially in a rock garden. It never flowers or berries, so the growth does not seem to have an adult stage.

■ RIGHT
'FILIGRAN'

A slow-growing sport of 'Boskoop' with fluted, nearly linear, forward-pointed lobes. Leaf blade and lobes are curled downwards. It makes a good houseplant.

■ LEFT
'EVA'

This self-branching ivy, selected from 'Harald' in Denmark in the 1960s, has small, pointed, three-lobed leaves with green and cream-yellow variegations. Grow it in loam-based compost (soil mix) for particularly good gold colouring. 'Eva' makes a good hanging basket and specimen plant, and is very good as a houseplant. It can also be used in making a bottle garden (terrarium), as the leaves are so neatly formed.

■ BELOW

'FLUFFY RUFFLES'

This is a most unusual, attractive, curly ivy. It has crimped, wavy-edged, five-lobed leaves, looking rather like round pompoms. The newest leaves have a pink tinge. It does best in hanging baskets, in a cold greenhouse or conservatory.

■ ABOVE

'GERTRUD STAUSS'

Introduced by the ivy nursery of Gerba Stauss, in Germany. This ivy has a medium-sized, five-lobed leaf, the centre lobe often divided to give a seven-lobed leaf. It is mid-green with grey-green blotches, with pale cream irregular variegation at the leaf edge. Good for hanging baskets and as edging in window boxes.

■ LEFT

'FANTASIA'

Thought to be a sport of 'Pittsburgh Variegated', this has a typical ivy-shape leaf, with three to five lobes. New growth is white to cream, with evenly-scattered green speckles and blotches. The main veins are white and remain so, even when the rest of the leaf turns green with age. It is best as an indoor plant or in a cool greenhouse.

■ RIGHT
'GOLDCHILD'

This is a lovely golden sport from
'Harald'. It was selected in Denmark
and given its name by Tom Rochford,
a leading houseplant nurseryman, in
honour of his new grandchild. It has a
particularly good colour: the medium-
sized leaves are yellow and three- to
five-lobed; the bottom lobes are very
shallow and the middle lobe is the
longest, pointed with a grey-green
centre marking. Sometimes the leaves
are completely yellow.

'Goldchild' was sold as a houseplant,
but it has proved itself hardy enough to
survive cold winters in both unheated
tunnels (cold greenhouse) and outside
in the garden. It is particularly good in
hanging baskets or growing up a fence.
A fast grower, if potted into loam-based
compost (soil mix), you should be able
to take cuttings after six months.

■ LEFT
'GLACIER'

This old self-branching ivy from the United
States is a very good silver-grey, variegated
cultivar. It is short-jointed but can grow quite
high. It usually fails to turn adult, but some of
the leaves can get quite large. The medium-
sized leaves are three- to five-lobed, with
shallow sinuses that make the leaf look almost
heart-shaped. They are grey-green in colour,
with silver-grey blotches and white edges.

'Glacier' is a reliable all-round ivy and
makes a good houseplant. It is a hardy plant
and is equally good planted in the garden
as ground cover, growing up walls, and in
hanging baskets, or in any other situation
where a hardy, silver leaf is required.

■ RIGHT
'GOLDEN INGOT'

This attractive Danish ivy is self-branching, and has medium-sized, five-lobed leaves with shallow sinuses. It is golden yellow with lime-green blotches and splashes, and a dark green edge. It is best used in indoor hanging baskets.

■ LEFT
'GOLDHEART'

This is a very popular ivy, though its origin is unknown. It has had many names, among them 'Oro di Bogliasco' and 'Jubilee'. The medium-sized leaves are green with yellow centres. Even on a wall with little sun, it keeps its colour, which is unusual for a variegated ivy. It occasionally sports a green shoot, especially if grown in acid soil. Always cut out green shoots as close as possible to the main stem.

'Goldheart' is a very hardy plant. It is best as a wall ivy, but it also makes a very good specimen plant if trained up a pole to about 1.5m (5ft) high, though it has a tendency to grow adult foliage and should be pruned hard once a year to prevent this. However, some older plants may grow as high as 2.4m (8ft) without turning adult.

■ RIGHT
'GREEN RIPPLE'

The shiny, medium-sized, dark green
leaf has three to five forward-pointing
lobes with predominantly raised veins.
It is a good, hardy and vigorous plant
for ground cover, growing up walls,
or fronting a window box.

■ BELOW
'IRA'

The leaves have three to five rounded
lobes, the lower lobes being almost
non-existent, and have irregular green
and yellow splashes all over. Best
grown as a houseplant.

■ ABOVE
'IVALACE'

The small, shiny, dark green leaves are
five-lobed, and the margins are finely
crimped. The young branches are freely
produced, and grow upright until about
18cm (7in) long. Makes a good bushy
pot plant and a successful garden ivy
for use as ground cover, over low walls,
and in hanging baskets.

■ LEFT
'JERSEY DORIS'

This ivy from the island of Jersey, United Kingdom, has typical ivy leaves with five broad lobes as wide as they are long. New growth is creamy white with pretty speckles and blotches of green, sometimes becoming mottled. The old leaves are green all over. Grow in good light for best results. Best suited for a border or up a wall.

■ RIGHT
'JUBILEE'

The small leaves are grey-green and white, giving the plant a silvery appearance, and pink-tinged in cold weather. They have three shallow lobes, and can appear triangular in shape. 'Jubilee' is a fairly hardy plant, and grows densely but slowly. It is a very popular ivy for houseplants, hanging baskets and as a border edging plant.

■ ABOVE
'KOLIBRI'

An attractive, good houseplant, sometimes confused with
'Schäfer Three'. It is a sport of 'Ingrid', and has small,
light green leaves with white or cream edges and flecks
and occasional grey-green blotches.

■ ABOVE
'KNÜLCH'

This ivy has dull green, almost rounded
leaves, with an irregular edge that is
distorted and gnarled. This ivy grows
best outside, and is used as an edging
plant for a path or border.

■ RIGHT
'LITTLE LUZII'

This is the dwarf form of 'Luzii', and is
a lovely bushy houseplant, its smaller
size making it more useful in the
home than 'Luzii'. It grows outwards
instead of upwards, and planted in
an ornamental pot can look very
attractive as a feature plant.

■ RIGHT
'LUZII'

This ivy originated at the Ernest Luz nursery in Stuttgart Fellbach, in Germany, and was first exhibited in 1951. It is a very good clone – although the leaf is gold-based and freckled all over in green, the colour remains constant and reliable, which it does not with other similar clones. Grow it in loam-based compost (soil mix). The leaves are three-lobed and generally medium-sized, though some are quite large; the stems are red-bronze and trail well. The trailing foliage is good for cutting or flower arranging. It is suitable for hanging baskets and for fronting window boxes. It grows well against a wall outside, and rarely turns adult.

■ ABOVE
'MAPLE LEAF'

A good, vigorous garden plant, 'Maple Leaf' has large green, glossy, five-lobed leaves, with some of the long narrow lobes having coarse teeth. It is short-jointed but trailing, and looks splendid growing up a wall or trellis.

■ RIGHT
'MANDA'S CRESTED'

Mutated from 'Merion Beauty' in the United States around the time of World War II, this was the first curly ivy. The medium-sized to large, light green leaves have five forks that curl downwards, and wavy edges. On well-grown plants, the leaves tend to be larger. Grown up tall canes, it soon makes a very good ivy pillar, for use as an architectural feature in the garden. Alternatively, grow it in hanging baskets, trained up a trellis or as a houseplant. In winter, this ivy turns a lovely bronze colour.

■ RIGHT
'MELANIE'

'Melanie' is a mutation from 'Parsley Crested' found at the Beth Chatto Nursery in Essex, England, in 1980. It was named after the member of staff who found it. The clone is quite stable. The leaves are five-lobed and ovate to rounded. They are generally light green with prominent green veins, and in warm weather the edges become undulating and crested, and tinged with deep red. 'Melanie' is not a vigorous grower and is best as a houseplant, though it will also do well outdoors if protected from extreme cold. It looks especially good covering long, low walls.

■ LEFT
'MERION BEAUTY'

This ivy, with small green, three- to five-lobed leaves, is an old sport of 'Pittsburgh'. Compact plants, bushy and self-branching, they make a mound of foliage when planted outside. 'Merion Beauty' is a bit small for the garden border, and is best on a rockery or as a houseplant.

'MIDAS TOUCH'

This ivy was raised by the Frode Maegaard Hedera Nursery of Ringe in Denmark. It was eventually registered as 'Midas Touch'. The leaves are three-lobed, heart-shaped, basically dark green with patches of lighter green, and irregularly marked with blotches of yellow. It makes a good pot plant and is suitable for hanging baskets, but can get wind-scorched in an exposed position.

'MINTY'

Originally called 'Mint Kolibri', but shortened to 'Minty' as this houseplant is not related to the true 'Kolibri'. Small leaves are three- to five-lobed, with lime-green spreading inwards from the edges, and blue-green splashes in the centre.

'OLIVE ROSE'

A sport from 'Très Coupé', 'Olive Rose' was introduced by Fibrex Nurseries, United Kingdom, in 1981. The small, mid- to light green, three-lobed leaves are variable in shape, with heavy cresting on the edges and surface. A rare and unusual plant, it can be grown outside in the border or as a climber, but does best as a houseplant.

■ RIGHT
'PARSLEY CRESTED'

This is an attractive ivy with rounded, light green, medium-sized to large leaves that turn a beautiful bronze outside in cold weather. The leaves are sometimes three-lobed but not conspicuously so, because of the raised cresting all around the edge of the leaf. This makes it resemble curly parsley. The long, strong-growing trailing stems make this a good ivy for flower arranging. In summer, plants grown up a trellis can be tied in at the top and allowed to hang down freely, enabling long, straight sprays to be cut. 'Parsley Crested' can be used in any way as an outdoor plant, but needs plenty of room as an indoor plant. It looks good in a conservatory, growing up a pillar or growing over an archway.

■ LEFT
'PEDATA'

This ivy was first called 'Caenwoodiana' in 1863, but without a description, so when Shirley Hibberd renamed it 'Pedata' with a description, that name took priority. The leaves are dark green with grey-white veins. They have five narrow lobes, the centre one being the longest, and the lateral ones appearing at right angles to it. Grow this hardy plant against a wall for best results.

■ RIGHT

'PERKEO'

The leaf is small to medium-sized, round
to heart-shaped, and unlobed. Its surface
is heavily puckered and light green,
turning mid-green with age. Cold
conditions turn the leaves light red,
making it an unusual-looking ivy.
'Perkeo' is a good houseplant, but it
looks best in cool conditions, such
as in a cold greenhouse or conservatory.

■ ABOVE

'PITTSBURGH'

This ivy is shown here so that you can see the plant that all the
self-branching, non-flowering American ivies descend from. It is
a typical-looking ivy, with medium-sized, three- to five-lobed,
pointed leaves, branching out vigorously from all leaf joints.
One cannot help wondering how so many attractive ivies, with
such diverse foliage, ever came from such a plain-looking plant.

■ RIGHT

'PERLE'

A sport from 'Harald'. The short-jointed, trailing habit makes
this ideal for hanging baskets. It has medium-sized, unlobed
leaves, which are mid-green with cream variegation at the leaf
edge. Pointed lobes may appear, but these are best trimmed off.

■ RIGHT
'ROMANZE'

A sport from 'Luzii', 'Romanze' was
selected by Brother Heieck and named
by him in 1979. The curly leaves
resemble 'Manda's Crested', but have
a faint mottle within the apple-green
colouring. The leaves are five-lobed and
deeply fluted, very curly, variegated gold
with green speckles all over. 'Romanze'
is only suitable as an indoor plant.

■ ABOVE
'SAGITTIFOLIA VARIEGATA'

The name describes a green and yellow, variegated, self-
branching ivy with a leaf shape reminiscent of a bird's foot.
Confusingly, it is a variegated form not of 'Sagittifolia' but
of 'Königers Auslese', owing to a nomenclature hiccup. This
golden variegated plant is extremely attractive, and is ideal for
hanging baskets and as a specimen pot plant. It is also good at
the front of a window box, cascading over the edge. It needs
plenty of light to ensure its colour remains a good yellow.

■ ABOVE
'SCHÄFER THREE'

This houseplant has been called several names in the past, as it
is somewhat unstable. Usually five-lobed, self-branching and
variegated, the small leaves are blotched in shades of dark green
and grey-green, with irregular streaks of white.

■ LEFT

'SILVER KING'

This dense-growing ivy has a small, five-lobed silver leaf. The central lobe is twice as long as the lateral lobes. It is a good grower outside, and is also ideal as a pot plant or window box.

■ BELOW

'TRITON'

This is a most unusual, eye-catching plant. It does not climb, but branches and sprawls, with medium-sized, deeply cut, forward-pointing, five-lobed leaves. The three centre lobes are longer and twisted. Dark green and shiny, it looks fantastic grown in a hanging basket or as a short specimen plant in a pot. The variegated form is called 'Spectre'.

■ LEFT

'SPETCHLEY'

This is the smallest ivy available, hence its earlier name, 'Minima'. Its small, three-lobed variable leaves, sometimes triangular, grow very densely. One of its main attractions is that the foliage changes with the first frost to a lovely wine colour. 'Spetchley' is a really hardy ivy. It grows best outdoors, either in a container or in the open garden (it will cover a wide area in a limestone rockery). It is not suitable as a houseplant.

Care and maintenance

The Grower's Guide

Ivies growing outdoors in garden soil require little maintenance. Once they are well established, they do not require regular watering, and need feeding only occasionally.

Ivies need annual trimming to keep them in shape, to restrict size, and to ensure that they do not turn adult if you require them to show only their juvenile form. Trim them over in spring, to remove any winter debris and damaged leaves. If they are growing against a wall, cut them back flat against its surface. At the same time, shorten the ivy's height to ensure that the plant will not grow anywhere near the eaves of a building. Ivy looks a bit bare following a trim, but after about six weeks it will return to its former splendour.

When growing ivies in containers outdoors, top-dress with a general feed two or three times a year. Trim and water in spring as well.

If you are growing ivy as a houseplant, it is vital to ensure that the soil does not dry out, since a hot, dry atmosphere can restrict growth and encourage red spider mite and scale aphids. To freshen up the foliage, spray the leaves with water once or twice daily using a hand spray. For extra protection, stand the ivy plant inside another pot on

a 2.5cm (1in) layer of sand and gravel. Watering the gravel on a weekly basis will keep the atmosphere around the plant moist, and may eliminate the need for spraying.

If the plant is growing in soilless compost (planting mix), it will need feeding once a month as well, using a houseplant feed. If it has been potted in loam-based compost (soil mix), this is not so essential.

A quick trim about every six weeks will keep the houseplant ivy in shape. Ivy may be trained to grow upright or left to trail, or a combination of the two. To train ivy to grow upwards, simply insert three canes into the pot and tie the stems to the canes. You can soon alter how the plant grows when you see how it suits its position.

■ ABOVE
The traditional spot for growing ivies is against a wall. A single ivy or a mixture of golden-leaved and darker, green-leaved ivies, are highly effective and need only a little regular care to look wonderful. Plant the ivies with enough space to allow for trimming between the plants.

Tree ivies

A tree ivy is highly decorative, but is not a natural plant form, and so requires considerable input from the gardener. Tree ivies consist of the adult form of ivy trained into a standard or free-standing shrub, up to 1–2m (4–7ft) tall: from soil level to two-thirds of the finished height of the whole plant, the stem is bare; the top third is taken up with a large, ball-like head of foliage, which is then kept in shape by regular pruning.

When selecting ivies for training into a standard, bear in mind that only certain species or cultivars can be used successfully: many cultivars keep their juvenile form and do not turn adult, and so will neither grow into a shrub shape, nor produce the berries which will make the tree so attractive. If unsure, check with your local nursery for the best choice.

Training a potted ivy

The main problem with growing tree ivies is that adult ivy is naturally shrubby and slow-growing, and is not inclined to grow a long, straight stem. If you are fortunate enough to have a potted plant that has already become adult and has a suitably long stem, then the process is fairly straight-forward. Just insert a cane into the pot, slightly longer than the required eventual height of the plant, and tie the stem at intervals of 10–15cm (4–6in) up the cane, right up to the joint beneath the adult shoot. Then, cut away all the other shoots, leaving one main stem tied to a cane with the adult shoot. In two to three years, it will develop into a bushy head, which will flower and berry each year.

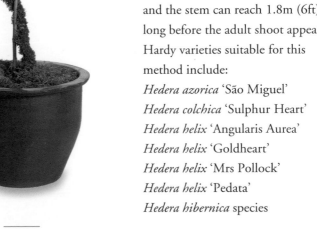

Remove the flowers to prevent the berries forming until the head is in the right proportion to the stem.

Growing from cuttings

If you don't have a plant already growing in a pot as described, you could grow the tree ivy from cuttings. Always take cuttings from an ivy in its juvenile form, and from a plant that is likely to turn adult within a reasonable time (see below). When rooted, pot them into 9cm (3½in) pots using a loam-based compost (soil mix). Once established, tie the main stem to a cane, then pot on into a 15cm (6in) pot until the single stem reaches 1.5m (5ft), cutting away any side shoots. To encourage the ivy to turn adult, give it plenty of light. The maturing process can take three to four years, and the stem can reach 1.8m (6ft) long before the adult shoot appears. Hardy varieties suitable for this method include:

Hedera azorica 'São Miguel'
Hedera colchica 'Sulphur Heart'
Hedera helix 'Angularis Aurea'
Hedera helix 'Goldheart'
Hedera helix 'Mrs Pollock'
Hedera helix 'Pedata'
Hedera hibernica species

Grafting

Another way to grow an ivy tree is to graft an adult ivy on to a well-grown juvenile shoot, which has been grown to the height you require. This is difficult, because adult ivy is very slow-rooting, but if you are good at grafting you could expect a 50 per cent success rate. This type of ivy tree was very popular in Victorian times, when gardeners were not in such a hurry to see results (the process often taking two to three years). This length of time is why this method is not a commercial proposition, and explains why such plants are not available at garden centres.

Plaiting ivy stems

This final method is recommended because it is reasonably quick. First, take three young, single-stemmed ivy plants in juvenile form with pliable stems; they will probably be about nine months old and of large-leaved varieties. Next, take a broom handle or 2m (7ft) length of cane which has been previously painted with a wood preservative and left for one week to dry. Insert the broom handle or cane vertically into a pot full of loam-based compost (soil mix), and plant the three ivies around it. Twine the growths around the stick, then tie them in. Remove the lower leaves as far from the base as required. As the stems grow, continue tying them in

GROWING TREE IVIES: THE PLAITING METHOD

1 Choose an ivy that has pliable stems, such as *Hedera marrocana* 'Spanish Canary', used here, and select three young but well-established, long-stemmed plants. Insert a broom handle or cane into a pot full of loam-based compost (soil mix) and place the plants evenly around its base.

2 Working your way up slowly, wrap the stems around the broom handle or cane, tying the stems together with twists at even intervals, to create a plaited effect.

3 As you get higher up the broom handle or cane, take care to check that the stems cross each time in a straight line above the previous crossed stems, and that even spacing is maintained throughout.

■ BELOW RIGHT

In a few years' time, when the supporting cane has rotted away, the plaited stems of this *Hedera helix* 'Lalla Rookh' tree ivy will be thick enough and strong enough to support themselves.

until they are within 25cm (10in) of the top of the broom handle or cane. From this point onwards, take no more leaves off. Instead, allow the leafy stems to reach the top of the broom or cane, then pinch out the growing points to prevent the plant from growing further, and to encourage growth from the leaf joints. Place a hanging basket on top of the broom handle or cane and secure. When the ivy side-shoots start to grow, gently feed them through the basket, training them until the outside of the basket is completely covered with ivy.

Plaited tree ivies can look very impressive in a conservatory or outside on the patio. A heavy clay pot provides added stability. Suggested ivies for this method are:

Hedera algeriensis 'Gloire de Marengo'
Hedera helix 'Adam'
H. helix 'Goldchild'
H. helix 'Luzii'
H. helix 'Sagittifolia Variegata'

4 Take a 25cm (10in) wire hanging basket and place it on top of the broom handle or cane, upside down, and secure in place with staples or nails.

5 Wind the tops of the shoots through the wire basket, and snip off all the lower leaves using scissors. As the ivy continues to grow, feed the shoots through the basket, covering the frame completely.

Ivy topiary

Topiary is a highly striking garden art form, and makes an elegant feature outdoors or in a conservatory. There are three main ways to create ivy topiary: the multiple stuffed method for three-dimensional topiary; using wire frames for two-dimensional shapes; and hanging baskets for creating topiary balls.

Three-dimensional topiary

The 'multiple stuffed method' is suitable for large and small designs or sculptures. Bold, impressive topiary specimens – elephants, giraffes, bears, deer, cows, birds and even people and objects, such as cars – may be created using this method. These are often seen in parks and gardens in the United States.

To create three-dimensional topiary, make a framework of wire, steel or wood for the skeleton of the shape (ready-made frames in different shapes are available in some garden shops). Cover the shape with wire netting, then line it with moss, just as you would line a hanging basket, leaving a hole through which to work. Through the hole, fill the structure with soilless compost (planting mix), then seal over the hole with more moss. Plant rooted

ivy cuttings all over the body, through the moss.

If you want to try this topiary, it is a good idea to begin with a small object before you try to make anything too elaborate, such as an elephant or giraffe.

Two-dimensional shapes

The 'wire frame' method is more suitable for flatter, two-dimensional objects. The skeleton frame, which has wire legs at the base for anchorage, is set in a compost-filled pot or container. Ivies are planted in the compost, and as they grow, their

shoots are gradually wrapped around the wire and cut to shape as they cover the frame.

A good place to start is to make a simple but very pretty flat heart-shaped sculpture. You should be able to buy a solid, ready-made heart-shaped frame, with wire legs at the base, from most nurseries. Fill a 43cm (17in) flower pot with loam-based compost (soil mix), firm it in, then place the wire legs of the heart-shaped frame into the top of the soil in the pot. Plant two small green ivies with long trails behind the legs. Insert the canes to help steady the frame, attaching them to each side of the heart; they are only necessary until the ivies are growing well. Next, pull the ivy stems through the front of the heart, and twine each trail separately up the wires. As the trails grow, wind them still further, going up and down until there is no bare wire showing.

The wire frame method does not, of course, give the same appearance as a free-standing object that is achieved with the multiple stuffed method, but often the topiary can be placed in a position where the base is hidden from sight. Topiary made this way is also much simpler to make and maintain, and will have a longer life than 'stuffed' topiary.

MAKING A CONICAL TOPIARY: THE WIRE FRAME METHOD

1 Take a pot large enough to accommodate your chosen frame, place drainage material in the base, and fill with loam-based compost (soil mix).

2 Plant seven small ivy plants with long trails (here, *Hedera helix* 'Ardingly') around the edge of the flower pot at even intervals.

3 Take your chosen topiary frame (here, a large cone), and gently place it in the pot, securing it carefully with your hands into the soil.

4 Carefully tease out each trail of ivy, and wind them up the sides and around the struts of the frame. Secure them with ties.

5 Pinch out all the growing tips and tuck the ends in. This will help to encourage side shoots and bushy growth, which will cover the frame.

6 Keep the topiary in shape by trimming when needed, using sharp scissors or shears. Push a long cane through the centre of the shape to help keep it steady, if necessary, until well-established.

Ivy topiary balls

One of the easiest ways of making an attractive ivy topiary is to train rooted cuttings around two hanging basket frames, which are then assembled to make a ball.

For this method you will need 100 rooted ivy cuttings, two 30cm (1ft) hanging baskets, a flower pot, and moss and soilless compost (planting mix) to fill the baskets.

Line each hanging basket with moss, using the flower pot for balance, fill with soilless compost and firm in. Secure the two baskets together, making a ball which is ready to plant. Next, make a 'planting peg' from a piece of wood, sharpening the point with a knife, and, starting from the top, make holes all over the moss, going round and round, and planting as you go.

Hang up the topiary ball and spray it all over with water; leave it to settle in a sheltered spot or in a cold greenhouse for a couple of weeks. Spray every day, and leave it out in a rain shower if possible.

Snip out the top of each cutting to make it grow bushy, and keep the ball under glass during winter, placing it outside after the danger of frost has passed.

GROWING IVY TOPIARY BALLS

1 Place one wire hanging basket on top of a flower pot for balance. Line the inside with moistened moss.

2 Fill with a soilless compost (planting mix), pressing down firmly. Repeat the process with the second hanging basket frame.

Caring for ivy topiary

Keep topiary plants well watered, and spray stuffed topiary and topiary balls daily in dry weather. It is vital to ensure that they do not dry out. Once a topiary design is established, it will need regular trimming to maintain its shape, using scissors or garden shears. Do not wait until the spring to cut back, as some growth will occur in the winter. In spring, it may be necessary to prune as often as fortnightly. After two months, give topiary a liquid feed every 10 days to keep it in good condition.

SUITABLE *HEDERA HELIX* VARIETIES FOR USE IN IVY TOPIARY

H. helix 'Adam'

H. helix 'Anita'

H. helix 'Ira'

H. helix 'Ivalace'

H. helix 'Jubilee'

H. helix 'Kolibri'

H. helix 'Merion Beauty'

H. helix 'Minty'

H. helix 'Silver King'

H. helix 'Ursula'

H. helix 'William Kennedy'

3 Place the two basket frames firmly together, and tie together at intervals with wire twists.

4 Using a sharpened peg or cane, poke holes in the moss and plant the cuttings (here *Hedera helix* 'Ivalace'), in a circular direction, starting from the top.

5 Once you have planted most of the cuttings, hang the basket up and finish the underside of the topiary ball, filling in any gaps.

■ LEFT AND ABOVE
There are many shapes of simple topiary frames to choose from – including heart and club shapes, and ball shapes – which are easy to construct. Start with simple designs before embarking on a more complicated three-dimensional shape.

Ivy hanging baskets

These are particularly useful if you want hanging baskets for the winter and spring, since ivies are the only hardy evergreens that trail. Because there is not much soil in a hanging basket, it is possible that in very severe weather the root balls can freeze; when that threatens, you must give them shelter in a garden shed or garage, returning them to their outside situation as soon as possible – do not make them tender by pampering. If standing the hanging basket on the ground or on concrete,

place it on sheets of newspaper, a sack or an old rug, to prevent the ivies from freezing to the ground.

To assemble your own hanging basket you will need one 35cm (14in) basket, enough damp moss to line the basket, loam-based compost (soil mix), and a selection of ivies and flowering plants.

Starting in early autumn, line the basket with moss and fill it with compost (the loam base produces more robust plants). Take five ivies from 9cm (3½in) pots and place them

COMBINATION IDEAS

• 5 *Hedera helix* 'Glacier', 5 dwarf pink tulips, 4 dwarf winter-flowering pansies
• 5 *Hedera helix* 'Ivalace', 5 pink forget-me-nots, 6 red dwarf wallflowers
• 5 *Hedera helix* 'Luzii', 7 dwarf yellow narcissi, 4 blue forget-me-nots
• 5 *Hedera helix* 'Adam', 7 purple crocuses, 5 double daisies

around the basket, leaving the centre free. Pinch out the growing tips to promote bushy plants. In late autumn, place your choice of flowering plants, such as tulips or forget-me-nots, in the centre space, and one between each ivy.

Renovating baskets

Once the baskets have reached the end of their winter/spring display, it is time to renovate them for the summer. To do this, you will need a 45–50cm (18–20in) basket. Take down the old basket, remove the hanging wires and turn out the contents without breaking up the growing ball, like turning out a

■ OPPOSITE BELOW LEFT

These pansies, daffodils and polyanthus have another
two or three weeks blooming before they will need
replanting. The ivy itself can be used again.

freshly baked cake from its tin. Hang
up the old basket in the garden shed
ready for next winter and, taking the
new basket, line it with fresh moss
and a layer of new compost, pressing
hard so that it looks like a bird's nest
inside. Now take the old root ball,
remove and throw away the old moss
and old flowering plants or bulbs, and
place the cleaned-up root ball into the
newly prepared basket, arranging the
trails over the sides, and adding more
compost where needed. Now add
some new bedding plants such as
zonal pelargoniums, petunias,
fuchsias or even a mixture of all three.
Because you already have the ivies
growing well around your basket,
you will not need as many plants as
if you were starting from scratch.

There is never any need to cast
aside your ivies after just two seasons'
use, as they can always be used again
in other types of planting.

When the second season is over,
trim the trails back, turn the whole
root ball out of the basket, pull out
the old summer flowers and then,
using a spade, chop or pull apart the
ivy edging into three pieces. These
can then be used again in garden
planting, or potted up in separate
large pots or containers to grow
on as specimen pot plants.

PLANTING A HANGING BASKET

1 First line a hanging basket with a
moist moss, patting it down as you
go. Press the moss firmly over the sides
of the hanging basket before filling with
compost (soil mix).

2 If you want to plant a combination of
ivies and other plants, place the ivies
around the edge of the basket, leaving the
centre free for other plants. In this case,
only *H. helix* 'Goldfinger' is being planted,
so the basket is completely filled.

3 Once you have completed the basket,
water it thoroughly and leave it to
settle in a sheltered spot or cool greenhouse
for about two weeks before hanging.

4 When established, the basket will make
a very effective display without needing
any flowers. Allow the trails to grow down
over the sides, trimming them occasionally.

Ivies in containers and window boxes

Container-growing is very satisfying, especially if you only have a small garden area. There are many attractive, inexpensive containers, and even old boxes, tubs, bowls, baskets and buckets that can be used, since they will eventually be obscured by the cascading growth. Ivies make very good permanent edging in window boxes, and seasonal changes need only be made to the non-hardy plants, leaving the ivy growing over the front.

Planting in containers

Growing ivies in containers is not difficult. The planting method for ivies in containers is as follows. First, make sure there is a drainage hole or two in the bottom of the container, especially if you are using one that is not purpose-made. Then cover the bottom of the container with old brick rubble, broken-up polystyrene (Styrofoam) plant-trays, or even very coarse gravel to facilitate the drainage. Finally, add a layer of compost (soil mix), preferably loam-based.

Such a compost is recommended because it does not dry out too quickly, and the compost contains fertilizer that is long-lasting. Alternatively, soilless compost (planting mix) can be used, but its nutrients will only last for six weeks in a container, so regular weekly feeding will be necessary.

■ ABOVE RIGHT
White petunias combine beautifully with a variegated ivy, trained over a wire frame to give the display added height and elegance.

■ LEFT
Ivies can be successfully used on their own or as tall background plants, grown up long canes. When regularly pruned, they also provide a source of cuttings to help with future plantings.

Renovating containers

Top-dressing the container with a base fertilizer once every six months keeps the compost 'alive' for two years without having to change it. Even then, it can be renewed without disturbing the ivies by chopping the soil out around the plants; even if some of the ivy roots get removed, it will not matter. With careful regular top-dressing, it is not impossible for ivies to thrive in their containers for up to 10 years.

Every two years, with the help of an extra pair of hands, the ivies need to be turned out and some of the soil teased away from the root ball. This can be done quite easily using a pointed stick. The plants are then repotted into the same pot, but with fresh loam-based compost. Water well and trim the trails fairly short.

PLANTING A WINDOW BOX

1 If necessary, make drainage holes in the base of your window box, then place a layer of stones, brick rubble or coarse gravel in the bottom.

2 Add a layer of compost (soil mix), filling the window box up to within 10cm (4in) from the top. Place the ivy along the front edge of the window box.

3 Along the back row of the window box, place your other plants. In this case, *H. helix* 'Eclipse' is being planted with *Fuchsia* 'Double Carido'.

This should be done at the end of the winter. Then stand the pots in a sheltered, shady position so the plants do not suffer from wind damage until they recover. If you have a cold greenhouse, repotting can be done during the winter and the plants kept there until they recover. Either way, the ivy will soon develop lovely juvenile foliage.

To keep plants flowering throughout the summer, give them a weekly high potash feed.

■ RIGHT
H. helix 'Eclipse' and fuchsia plants make a pleasing and easily achieved display.

Year-round display

Small conifers and shrubs combine well with ivy for permanently planted containers. Always use a loam-based compost (soil mix). Flowering plants can then be added and changed according to the season. Bulbs are excellent for early spring, but should be removed when they finish blooming, as the dying foliage is unattractive. Early spring primrose, English daisies and pansies are all ideal, followed by any of the range of summer bedding plants available.

■ LEFT AND BELOW LEFT
With a little thought, you can have lovely window boxes all year round. This display (left) of hyacinths, daisies and polyanthus is gently encased by this variegated ivy. For a winter display (below left), a mixture of polyanthus, conifers and ivy provide colour.

PERMANENT PLANTING COMBINATIONS

• Dwarf conifers with silver-leaved *Hedera helix* 'Glacier'
• *Aucuba japonica* 'Variegata' with *Hedera helix* 'Goldchild'
• *Buxus sempervirens* 'Suffruticosa' in the background with *Hedera helix* 'Ivalace'
• *Ligustrum ovalifolium* 'Aureum' with *Hedera helix* 'Luzii'
• *Lonicera nitida* 'Baggesen's Gold' with *Hedera helix* 'Goldfinger'

Propagation

The easiest way to propagate ivies is by taking stem cuttings. Propagation by seed is complicated, and has the added disadvantage that the characteristics of a clone are not usually transmitted by seed.

The quickest rooting comes from tip cuttings of juvenile foliage. Each should be about 5–8cm (2–3in) long, cut about 5mm (¼in) below a leaf joint. The cuttings should be inserted into a pot of moist loam-based compost (soil mix), planting six cuttings to a pot. A plastic bag covering the pot, and supported by a cane, forms a tent-like structure which will provide good conditions for rooting.

Stand the pot in a warm, shady place in the greenhouse, or on a windowsill. When rooted (which will take from four to six weeks), separate the cuttings, and then plant four to a 13cm (5in) pot or two to a 9cm (3½in) pot. A soilless compost (planting mix) can be used at this stage, as it is not permanent planting.

When the pot is full of roots, the ivy can be planted in the garden, after it has been hardened off. If it is to be grown as a pot plant, it should be potted up gradually into larger pots as the roots fill each container, always using a loam-based compost.

TAKING ROOT CUTTINGS

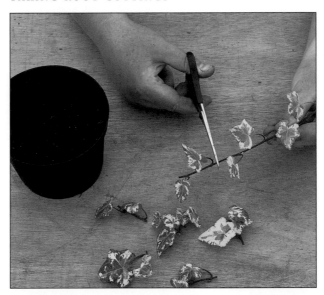

1 Using sharp scissors or secateurs (pruners), make small cuttings, each about 5–8cm (2–3in) long, from the tips of juvenile foliage. Here, *Hedera helix* 'Golden Ingot' has been used.

2 Insert the cuttings into a 13cm (5in) pot filled with moist loam-based compost (soil mix), planting six cuttings of ivy per pot.

3 Place the pot in a plastic bag, tying the top of the bag to a cane inserted into the middle of the pot. Leave in a warm, shady place for four to six weeks.

Pests and diseases

■ BELOW
The leaves of *H. colchica* are quite striking, but take care not to overwater, which increases the possibility of brown spot.

Ivies are fairly healthy, strong-growing plants, and are rarely troubled by pests. Their tenacious growth and ability to make a good show usually commends them to the amateur gardener. Their worst enemy is red spider mite.

Aphids

How to identify: Blackfly and greenfly can occasionally infest the growing tips, causing stunted growth and excreting a substance called honeydew, which may then become covered with sooty mould.
Control and prevention: An aphid-specific insecticide can be used if aphids are a problem.

Red spider mite

How to identify: If your plants have been kept in dry sunny conditions and then the leaves start browning at the edges, look on the undersides of the leaves: if you see a browny dust, you probably have red spider mite.
Control and prevention: Proprietary insecticides are usually effective. In a greenhouse or conservatory, the pests may be pesticide-resistant, and in this situation it is possible to use a biological control. A predatory mite

called *Phytoseiulus persimilis*, available from specialist suppliers, is very effective. It usually has to be replaced each year; having killed all the red spider mite, the predator then starves to death. It is important to maintain humidity, so in hot weather, spray plants grown in the greenhouse or conservatory frequently with water.

Scale insects and leaf scale

How to identify: Scale insects are tiny, yellowy-brown flat insects found on the undersides of the leaves. They excrete honeydew, encouraging sooty mould on the top of the leaves.

On outdoor ivies, especially those growing on warm, dry walls, leaf scale can appear. Insects produce one generation a year, and in early summer they cover themselves with a white waxy substance in which they lay their eggs. Soft scale occurs on ivies that are under glass; the insects breed all year round, and lay eggs under their shells.
Control and prevention: For the outdoor variety, spray in mid-summer with malathion/insecticidal soap. The same treatment applies for soft scale, at any time when the pests appear, but you may need to spray several times at two-weekly intervals.

Diseases

How to identify: In commercial situations, where ivies are grown under highly specialized, intensive conditions, bacterial leaf spot and septoria root rot can occur. However, diseases are unlikely to affect ivies that have been grown in normal conditions. Occasionally, brown spots can appear on *Hedera algeriensis* and *H. colchica* varieties if they have been overwatered.
Control and prevention: In either situation, cut back affected parts of the plants and burn them. As a preventive measure if the problem persists, cut back all plants once a year and burn all the foliage. Growing all stock plants without heat will also improve their resistance.

Other recommended ivies

Hedera algeriensis
'Gloire de Marengo'

Hedera algeriensis
'Marginomaculata'

Hedera algeriensis
'Montgomery'

Hedera algeriensis
'Ravensholst'

Hedera algeriensis 'Gloire de Marengo'

Large, glossy green leaves with silver variegations all over. It is a vigorous grower, and has been used extensively in the houseplant trade all over the world for many years. Although it can be planted outside, preferably against a wall, it is not fully hardy, and needs winter protection.

Hedera algeriensis 'Marginomaculata'

Large, ovate leaves splashed with green and spotted with cream-yellow. Makes a very good pillar plant or house-plant and is not fully hardy.

Hedera algeriensis 'Montgomery'

Broadly ovate medium-sized leaves that are bright green in summer and bronze with green veins in winter. Will be damaged by severe frost. It is usually used as a houseplant, but will survive in a cold conservatory provided it is not too frosty.

Hedera algeriensis 'Ravensholst'

Large green, mostly three-lobed leaves. New growth is shiny dark green. The stems are an attractive wine-red. 'Ravensholst' is sometimes known as 'Elephant Ears' because of its large leaf, which can be as large as 18cm (7in) long and 14cm (5½in) wide. It is suitable for ground cover in mild climates, and makes a good houseplant where winters are severe.

Hedera azorica 'Pico'

Medium to large leaves. New leaves are light green and covered with minute hairs. Old leaves are barely three-lobed and dark matt green. Makes a striking specimen plant.

Hedera colchica 'Sulphur Heart'

Large, heart-shaped leaf with three forward-pointing lobes, and widely spaced 'teeth' at the edges. Green with light yellow-green irregular markings through the centre. Hardy and suitable for climbing over walls, fences and as a specimen plant.

Hedera cypria

Medium-sized, three-lobed, dark blackish green leaves with green veins. Found in the Troodos mountains of Cyprus. Good juvenile form. Excellent for walls or as a specimen plant.

Hedera helix 'Atropurpurea'

Medium-sized, black-purple leaves in winter – the lower the temperatures, the darker they become. The leaves revert to green in spring. Good against a wall.

Hedera helix 'Brokamp'

This is very similar to another ivy called *H. helix* 'Gavotte', but they are reputed to be from separate clones. 'Brokamp' has pointed, heart-shaped, medium-sized leaves in mid- to dark green, and is self-branching but with long, trailing, green-purple stems. It is suggested that for best results the stock should be grown in loam-based compost (soil mix) with added dolomite limestone, so that it gets enough lime to stabilize the plant and prevent reversion in its foliage. It makes good ivy pillars, and is also useful as a houseplant, in window boxes and hanging baskets, and for a wall where dense coverage is needed. When propagating, select only typical ivy-shaped, pointed foliage.

Hedera azorica 'Pico'

Hedera colchica 'Sulphur Heart'

Hedera helix 'Atropurpurea'

Hedera helix 'Ursula'

Hedera helix 'Ceridwen'
Similar to 'Goldchild' but smaller in size overall. Leaves are three- to five-lobed with yellow to gold edges and irregular green to light green and grey-green centres. Good as specimen plants in pots.

Hedera helix 'Chalice'
Stiff-stemmed, upright plant, with dark green, three- to five-lobed, medium-sized leaves which are very variable. Leaf edges are undulated and leaves are cupped upwards. Suitable as a houseplant.

Hedera helix 'Chester'
Medium-sized, three-lobed leaf with shallow sinuses, giving it an almost triangular appearance. Leaves are light green, irregularly variegated cream-yellow; some are completely yellow. Tall, quick-growing ivy good for growing up arches.

Hedera helix 'Chrysophylla'
An old adult variety of which there is no juvenile form. Medium-sized leaves are yellow or dark green. Often thought, incorrectly, to be the same as 'Spectabilis Aurea'. A lovely garden plant.

Hedera helix 'Golden Snow'
Medium, three-lobed leaves, sometimes with two vestigial lobes; mid-green with broken areas of grey-green. The white margin is broken up with pale yellow to gold. Suitable for baskets and containers.

Hedera helix 'Harald'
The medium-sized leaves are three- to five-lobed, with occasional vestigial basal lobes. The centres are grey-green, bordered irregularly with creamy white. It is a vigorous, popular houseplant, but needs good light to maintain its colour.

Hedera helix 'La Plata'
A compact bird's foot-type ivy with small, three-lobed leaves with basal lobes. The blunt tips are self-branching. This ivy makes a good houseplant.

Hedera helix 'Little Picture'
The leaves are deep green, small and curled. This ivy has bushy spreading habit, and is good for ground cover.

Hedera helix 'Little Witch'
The small to medium-sized leaves have three long, narrow, forward-pointing lobes, and are often divided; some are ovate, with scalloped edges. A good houseplant.

Hedera helix 'Marilyn'
A new introduction from Denmark selected from 'Golden Ingot'. The leaves are mostly five-lobed, flat and bright green with splashes of lemon to gold. Good for hanging baskets and containers.

Hedera helix 'Mariposa'
The medium-sized leaf has six to eight asymmetrical lobes with the terminal lobe split in two, giving it the appearance of a swallow-tailed butterfly. An ideal houseplant.

Hedera helix 'Mathilde'
Small to medium-sized leaves with five forward-pointing lobes. Variegated with grey-green and irregular creamy edges. Use in hanging baskets.

Hedera helix 'Mini Ester'
A very compact and self-branching ivy with small, three-lobed leaves with green to grey-green centres, this ivy is best suited to indoor use.

Hedera helix 'Minor Marmorata'
Has small to medium-sized, dark green leaves, each three-lobed with shallow sinuses. Spotted and splashed creamy white. Hardy outdoor climber.

Hedera helix
'William Kennedy'

Hedera hibernica 'Aracena'

Hedera hibernica 'Deltoidea'

Hedera hibernica 'Sulphurea'

Hedera helix **'Needlepoint'**
Small-leaved bird's foot ivy with three narrow lobes, but older stems become five-lobed with a pair of compact and bushy basal lobes. Prefers an indoor situation.

Hedera helix **'Nigra Aurea'**
Small, three-lobed leaves are dark green with yellow streaking, and turn blackish green in winter. Best grown outside on a low wall.

Hedera helix **'Paper Doll'**
A sport from 'Glacier'. The leaf has grey-shaded white colouring and a narrow white edge. Use in hanging baskets.

Hedera helix **'Pin Oak'**
A compact, self-branching ivy believed to be a sport of 'Königers Auslese'. The small bird's foot-type leaf is light green and three-lobed with rounded tips, making it an attractive houseplant ivy.

Hedera helix **'Poetica'**
Also known as Italian or poets' ivy, this is a very ancient plant. Its main distinction is that it has yellow berries instead of black, but it is slow to turn adult. It has five-lobed, light green, medium-sized leaves.

Hedera helix **'Professor Friedrich Tobler'**
Slender, medium green leaves, mostly split into three or five divisions, and looking quite unlike a typical ivy. The leaves turn bronze in cold weather. Strong-growing and good in hanging baskets.

Hedera helix **'Rüsche'**
A sport of 'Professor Friedrich Tobler'. The medium-sized mid-green leaves are three-lobed with deep sinuses. The lobes are wedge-shaped, often pointing downwards. A fast grower – use for ground cover.

Hedera helix **'Sally'**
This self-branching ivy has five broad lobes. In cool conditions, the new growth is creamy lemon splashed with lime-green. The leaves darken to mid-green as they age. It has medium-sized leaves and works well in window boxes.

Hedera helix **'Shamrock'**
This medium-sized, dark green, self-branching ivy is three-lobed, the centre lobe being wedge-shaped, with rounded tips. The lateral lobes overlap the centre lobe. It is a popular plant for topiary because it grows very densely, and it is also good for hanging baskets. It is reasonably hardy.

Hedera helix **'Silver Emblem'**
Small, grey-green leaf overlaid with cream, with three forward-pointing lobes. A pretty ivy for hanging baskets.

Hedera helix **'Spear Point'**
Small, three-lobed mid-green leaves with wedge-shaped bases. The terminal lobe is the longest, with two small forward-pointing lateral lobes. A good climbing ivy.

Hedera helix **'Stift Neuberg'**
Sharply variegated, the medium-sized white and green leaf is round and crinkled with pink stems. Very slow-growing, suitable as a houseplant.

Hedera helix **'Sunrise'**
Traditional, medium-sized, golden yellow ivy-shaped leaf. Good as a houseplant and for hanging baskets.

Hedera helix **'Très Coupé'**
This vigorous grower has a bushy habit and small, deeply cut, green leaves. Good as a houseplant, for topiary and hanging baskets, and for low walls and ground cover.

Hedera maderensis
subsp. *iberica*

Hedera maderensis 'Madeira'

Hedera nepalensis var.
nepalensis 'Suzanne'

Hedera nepalensis var. *sinensis*

Hedera helix 'Tricolor'
A very old British ivy. The
small leaves are blotched dark
green and grey-green, with a
pretty cream and pink edge,
which deepens in winter. It
never turns adult and is very
slow-growing. It is hardy, but
is best grown in a sheltered
position outside against a
wall, not as a houseplant.
Hedera helix 'Tripod'
Narrow, three-lobed,
medium-sized, mid-green
leaves. The central lobes
are longer than the lateral
lobes, which are set at right
angles. This ivy makes a
good houseplant.
Hedera helix 'Troll'
Like a miniature 'Triton',
with small three-lobed leaves,
the centre lobe being the
largest, in light to medium
green. Self-branching.
Good houseplant ivy.

Hedera helix 'Ursula'
Bright yellow-green, small
leaves, three-lobed, with a
slightly longer terminal lobe.
Good for ground cover and
hanging baskets.
Hedera helix 'Vera'
Three- to five-lobed,
medium-sized, green and
cream leaves. Self-branching,
trailing habit. Suitable for
hanging baskets.
Hedera helix 'White Knight'
A pretty houseplant, this has
three- to five-lobed leaves
with a large splash of white
in the centre and green edges,
and wine-coloured stems.
**Hedera helix 'William
Kennedy'**
Dense-growing ivy with small,
silver leaves with three blunt
lobes and a longer terminal
lobe. Mature foliage develops
two small basal lobes. Good
for hanging baskets.

Hedera helix 'Zebra'
Cream and green, medium-
sized leaf, heavily veined,
giving the leaf a striped
appearance. A houseplant ivy.
Hedera hibernica 'Aracena'
Generally unlobed leaves,
although may sometimes
be three-lobed. In the cold,
leaves turn black. Good for
outdoor container displays.
Hedera hibernica 'Deltoidea'
Commonly known as the
'Sweetheart' or 'Shield' ivy,
this makes a good specimen
plant. The blunt triangular
leaves sometimes overlap
at the base of the lobes.
Hedera hibernica 'Sulphurea'
Medium-sized, mostly
rounded leaves with three
shallow lobes. Gold-green
and puckered all over, with
irregular gold or silver edges.
Grow against a wall, but
needs tying in at planting.

Hedera maderensis
subsp. *iberica*
Medium-sized, bright green,
three-lobed leaf with centre
lobes nearly as long as the leaf
is wide. Prominent green
veins with red stems. A fast
grower – plant along walls.
Hedera maderensis 'Madeira'
Medium-sized, three-lobed,
occasionally five-lobed, green
leaves on vigorous stems.
A good outdoor climber.
Hedera nepalensis var.
nepalensis 'Suzanne'
Dark green, medium-sized,
three- to five-lobed leaf with
extended terminal lobe. Good
for growing up a pillar.
Hedera nepalensis
var. *sinensis*
Shiny green, medium, heart-
shaped leaves are wider than
they are long. New growth
and stems take on a reddish
colour. A lovely climber.

Index

■ LEFT
Ivy creates a pretty entrance-
way into this garden.

ACKNOWLEDGEMENTS
The publisher would like to
thank all the staff at Fibrex
Nurseries for their assistance
with this book. All the
pictures have been taken by
Jonathan Buckley, except the
following: Michelle Garrett 4;
Harry Smith Collection 7;
A–Z Botanical Collection
11br, 13tr, 15br; The Garden
Picture Library 12tr, 48; John
Freeman 13bl, 54bl; Debbie
Patterson 14bl; Marie O'Hara
52, 54tr, 56bl; Houses and
Interiors 56tr. Also by J.
Buckley: Private Garden,
Upper Shelderton, UK 3;
Great Dixter, East Sussex, UK
12bl; Shropshire UK 16br.

■ RIGHT
A mixture of golden and green
ivy looks striking against a wall.